astrotheatre

A revolutionary approach to the ancient art of astrology

AstroTheatre: A revolutionary approach to the ancient art of astrology
Copyright © 2021 by Michael Bartlett
All rights reserved
First Edition
ISBN for Print Edition: **978-0-578-33768-5**

Written by Michael Bartlett
Artwork by Christine Cianci
Edited by Heather Fessenden
This book may not be reproduced in whole or in part, in any form or by any means, electronic or mechanical, including photocopying, recording, or by any information storage and retrieval system now known or hereafter invented, without written permission from the publisher or author. Reviewers may quote brief passages.
Disclaimer: The imagery presented herein is not meant to represent any human being living or dead, but to convey a sense of each of the planets.
Publisher and authors are not liable for any typographical errors, content mistakes, inaccuracies, or omissions related to the information in this book.
Published by Astro-Core Publishing

Introduction to Astrology and AstroTheatre

Astrology is the study of the movement of the planets, Moon, asteroids and the Sun through time and space and their relationship to one another as well as to us, here on Earth. While astrology takes many years for a person to learn, my intention with this book is to give you the building blocks of astrology: the planets, zodiac signs and their houses in a **visual** manner so as to aid astrological awareness.

Several years ago, I came up with the idea of AstroTheatre (the app is available from Apple) which is a visual representation of astrology using the following building blocks:

Who? The planets as *actors*

How & What? The signs are the *costumes* the actor wears and the *tools* the actor uses

Where? The houses are the *stages* or *areas of life* where the actors act

We will look at each of these three groups over the course of the book using visual representations and key words to develop your understanding of astrology. Using the key words stated in this book, you can gain a basic understanding of an astrology chart. As your understanding of astrology and the meanings attached to planets, signs and houses grow so will your astrological vocabulary.

I want to give a special thanks to the artist who made this idea real. Every planet and sign were hand painted in oil by the amazing artist Christine Cianci (www.ccianciart.com).

Astrology – an overview of the planets

Known as the personal planets, these planets represent the more personal parts of our lives:

The Sun	☉	Ego
The Moon	☽	Emotions
Mercury	☿	Communication
Venus	♀	Beauty
Mars	♂	Action

Known as the social planets, these planets represent the ways in which we relate to others in the social areas of our lives:

Jupiter	♃	Expansion
Saturn	♄	Authority
Chiron	⚷	Teacher, educator, facilitator

Known as the transpersonal planets, these planets represent the ways in which we relate to the transpersonal and transcendental areas of our lives:

Uranus	♅	Shock/Change
Neptune	♆	Dream
Pluto	♇	Transform

We will begin by introducing our actors, the planets and their characteristics, then how they act and what they tend to do and use in the signs and then finally the stages where everything happens!

chapter one

Introducing our actors known as the Planets or wanderers

The Sun

Rules the sign Leo

The Sun represents:

- ◊ How you shine out and are seen by others
- ◊ The hero part in you
- ◊ The man or masculine image of yourself, whether male or female
- ◊ Your vitality
- ◊ Your father or authoritative parent
- ◊ The Animus in Jungian psychology
- ◊ Your ego
- ◊ The Sun is something you grow into over the course of your life.

the Moon

◆ Rules the sign Cancer

The Moon represents:

- ◊ Your emotional self
- ◊ Your mother or nurturing parent
- ◊ The body, especially if you are a woman
- ◊ The Anima in Jungian psychology
- ◊ The feminine image of yourself – whether male or female
- ◊ How you nurture and feel
- ◊ Your instinctual nature your family or tribal history

Mercury

Rules the signs Gemini and Virgo

Mercury represents:

- ◊ How you communicate
- ◊ How you think, process and analyze information
- ◊ How you move, your coordination, your nervous system
- ◊ How you access information from the unconscious to the conscious.

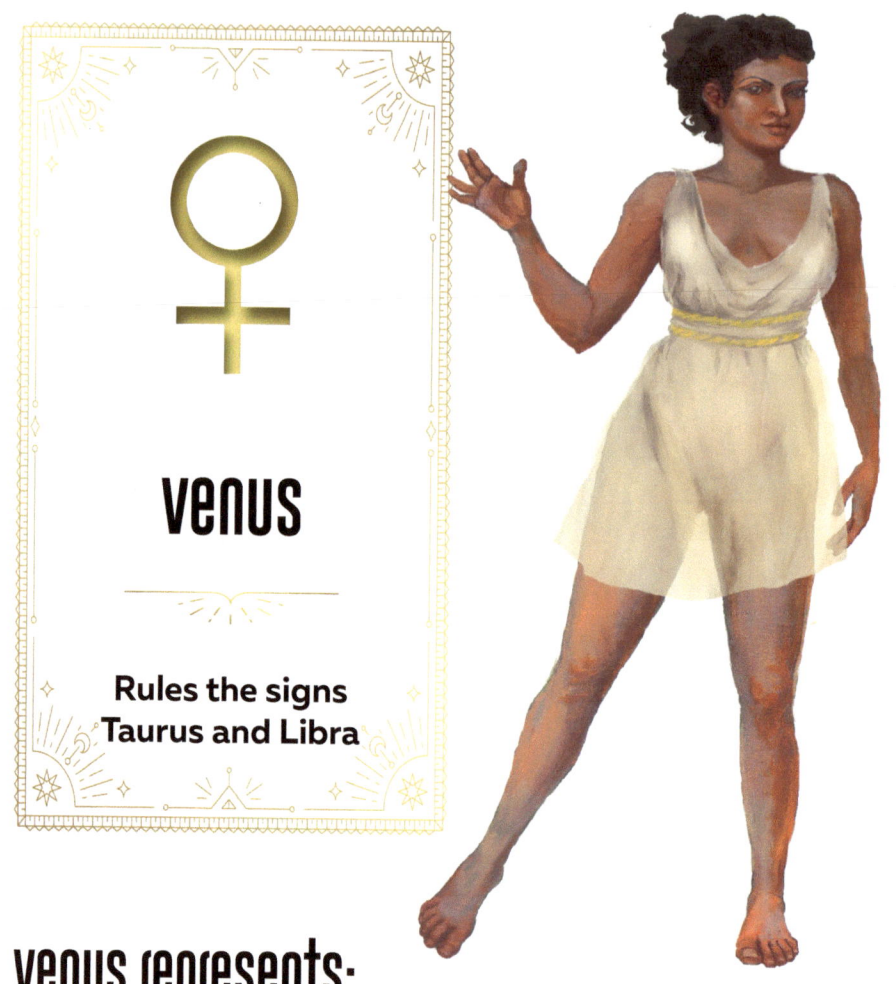

venus

Rules the signs Taurus and Libra

venus represents:

- ◊ How you perceive and experience:
    - Beauty
    - Love
    - Art
    - Relationships
- ◊ Your personal values
- ◊ How you relate to money
- ◊ Your personal resources
- ◊ How you relate to the feminine principle

Mars

Rules the signs Aries and Scorpio

Mars represents:

- ◊ How you need to be active (on many levels, but especially the physical)
- ◊ Your "drive" in life and often how you drive
- ◊ How you are courageous
- ◊ How you express your passion and desires

♃

Jupiter

Rules the signs Sagittarius and Pisces

Jupiter represents:

- How you grow and expand
- How you express your philosophies in life
- How you show and express your generosity
- How you show your joy

♄ saturn

Rules the signs Capricorn and Aquarius

saturn represents:

- How you structure
- How you experience authority, both your own and from others
- How you show and experience responsibility
- Your need for security
- How you experience discipline
- The hard lessons in life you have to learn

chiron

Chiron is an asteroid known as the wounded healer who heals

chiron represents:

- ◊ How you deal with the wound in your life you never think will go away

- ◊ Represents your need for healing and the area in your life where it needs to happen

- ◊ How you express your healer/educator/facilitator

- ◊ Through the wound(s) in your life, how you learn to be a better person and teach others about how to heal their own wounds/hurts

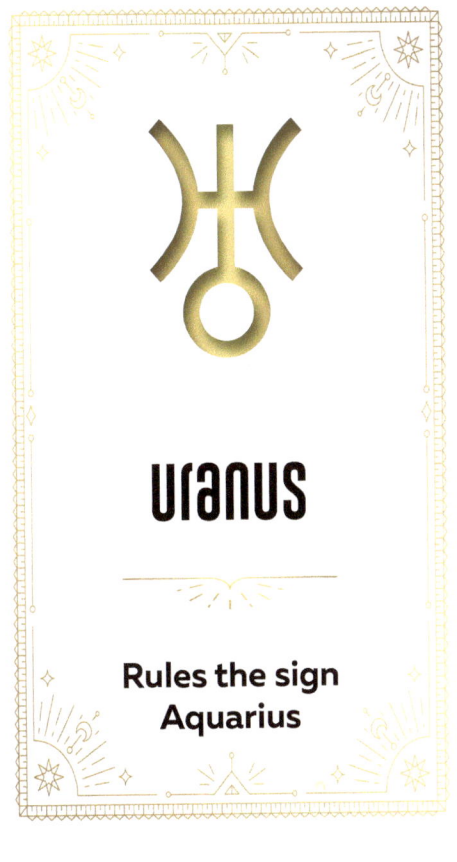

Uranus

Rules the sign Aquarius

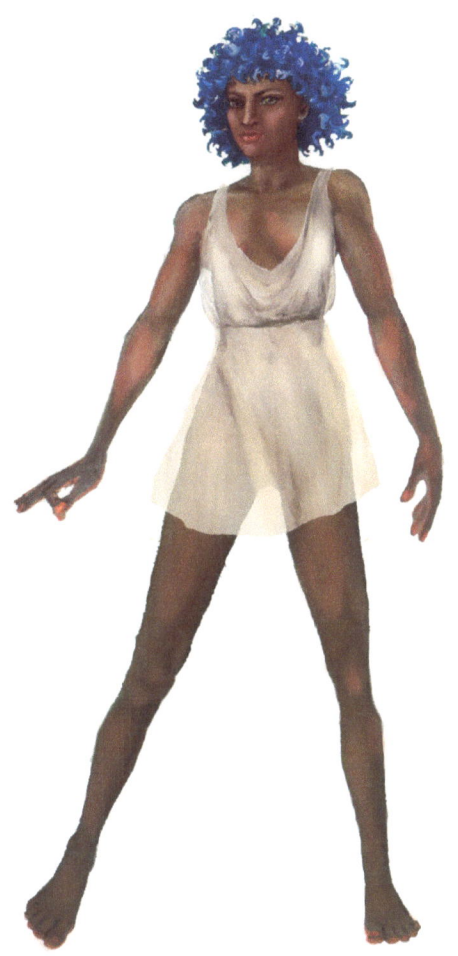

Uranus represents:

- ◊ Your need for the new and unexpected
- ◊ How you shock and evolve
- ◊ How and where you like to have fun
- ◊ Shows where in your life you like to change things
- ◊ Shows the area in life in which you may feel alienated

neptune

Rules the sign Pisces

neptune represents:

- ◊ How you "merge" with others
- ◊ Your need to connect through spirituality, creativity, imagination, dreaming
- ◊ How you escape reality through drugs, alcohol, movies
- ◊ Your spiritual heart

pluto

Rules the sign Scorpio

pluto represents:

- ◇ How and where you transform
- ◇ How you destroy for your highest good
- ◇ Where you are ruthless
- ◇ How you express phoenix-like ability
- ◇ Where you can go deep
- ◇ Your type of nuclear reactor

chapter two

Where we learn how our actors appear and the tools they like to use in the 12 astrological signs

Here we see how the Moon transforms herself through the clothing she wears and the tools she uses in each of the astrological signs. The key word for the Moon is to Feel.

Aries Moon

To Feel, Energetic, Assertive

Taurus Moon

To Feel, Patient, Earthy

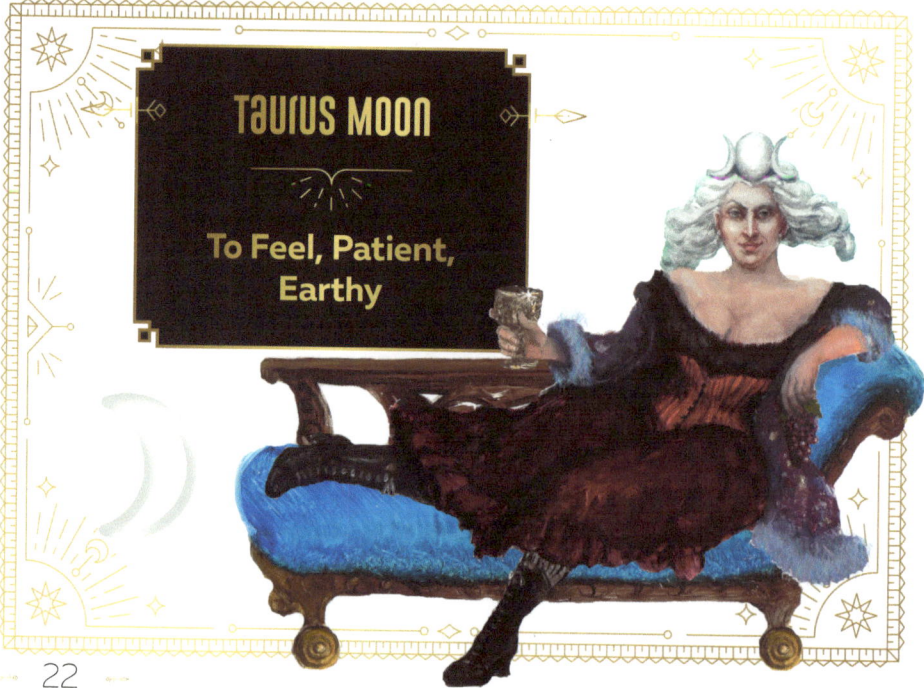

Gemini Moon

To Feel, Mobile, Mutable

Cancer Moon

To Feel, Nurturing, Emotional

Leo Moon

To Feel, Bold, Regal

Virgo Moon

To Feel, Careful, Precise

Libra Moon

To Feel, Relational, Balancing

Scorpio Moon

To Feel, Intense, Private

sagittarius moon

To Feel, Expansive, Buoyant

capricorn moon

To Feel, Structured, Disciplined

Aquarius Moon

To Feel, Tolerant, Progressive

Pisces Moon

To Feel, Intuitive, Poetic

Here we see how the Sun transforms himself through the clothing he wears and the tools he uses in each of the astrological signs. The key word for the Sun is to Shine.

Aries Sun

To Shine, Energetic, Assertive

Taurus Sun

To Shine, Patient, Earthy

Gemini Sun

To Shine, Mobile, Mutable

Cancer Sun

To Shine, Nurturing, Emotional

Leo Sun

To Shine, Bold, Regal

Virgo Sun

To Shine, Careful, Precise

Libra Sun

To Shine, Relational, Balancing

Scorpio Sun

To Shine, Intense, Private

sagittarius sun

To Shine, Expansive, Buoyant

capricorn sun

To Shine, Structured, Disciplined

Aquarius Sun

To Shine, Tolerant, Progressive

Pisces Sun

To Shine, Intuitive, Poetic

Here we see how Mercury transforms itself through the clothing it wears and the tools it uses in each of the astrological signs. The key word for Mercury is Communication.

Aries Mercury

Communication, Energetic, Assertive

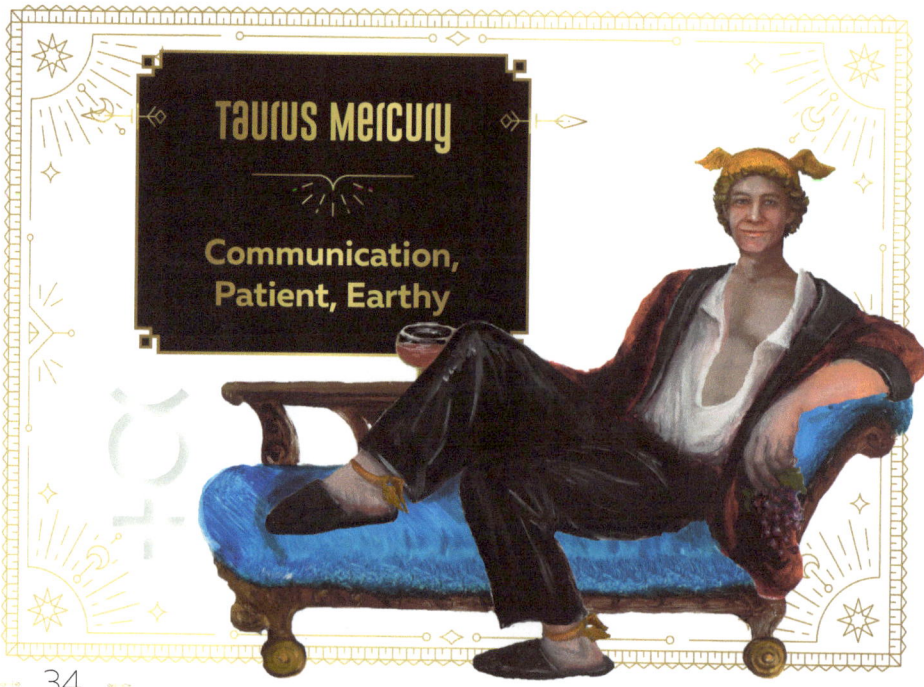

Taurus Mercury

Communication, Patient, Earthy

Gemini Mercury

Communication, Mobile, Mutable

Cancer Mercury

Communication, Nurturing, Emotional

Leo Mercury

Communication, Bold, Regal

Virgo Mercury

Communication, Careful, Precise

Libra Mercury

Communication, Relational, Balancing

Scorpio Mercury

Communication, Intense, Private

sagittarius Mercury

Communication, Expansive, Buoyant

capricorn Mercury

Communication, Structured, Disciplined

Aquarius Mercury

Communication, Tolerant, Progressive

Pisces Mercury

Communication, Intuitive, Poetic

Here we see how Venus transforms herself through the clothing she wears and the tools she uses in each of the astrological signs. The key word for Venus is to Love.

Aries Venus

Love, Energetic, Assertive

Taurus Venus

Love, Patient, Earthy

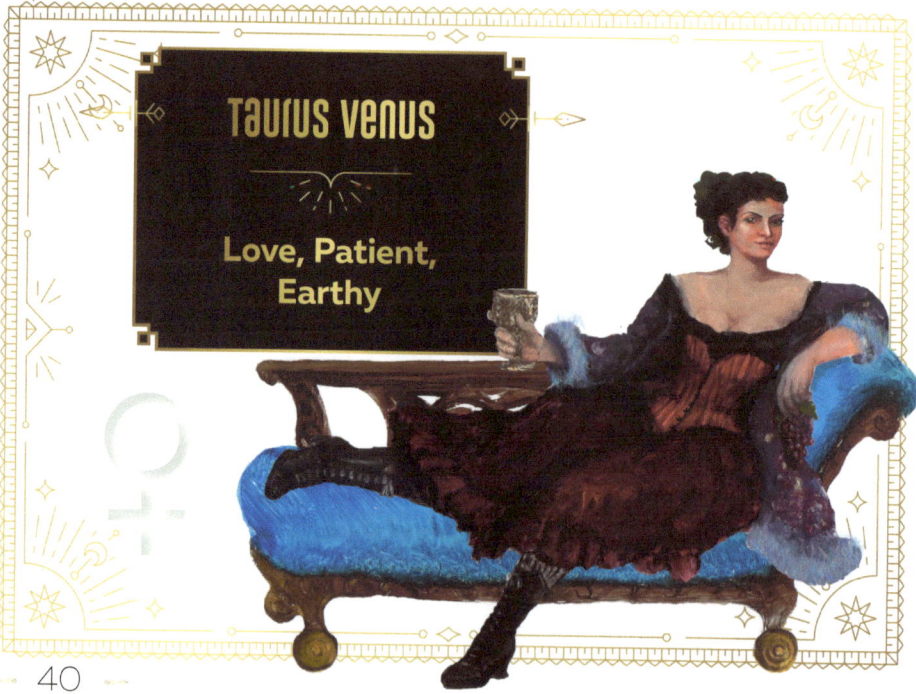

gemini venus

Love, Mobile, Mutable

cancer venus

Love, Nurturing, Emotional

Leo Venus

Love, Bold, Regal

Virgo Venus

Love, Careful, Precise

libra venus

Love, Relational, Balancing

scorpio venus

Love, Intense, Private

sagittarius venus

Love, Expansive, Buoyant

capricorn venus

Love, Structured, Disciplined

Aquarius Venus

Love, Tolerant, Progressive

Pisces Venus

Love, Intuitive, Poetic

Here we see how Mars transforms himself through the clothing he wears and the tools he uses in each of the astrological signs. The key word for Mars is Strength.

Aries Mars

Strength, Energetic, Assertive

Taurus Mars

Strength, Patient, Earthy

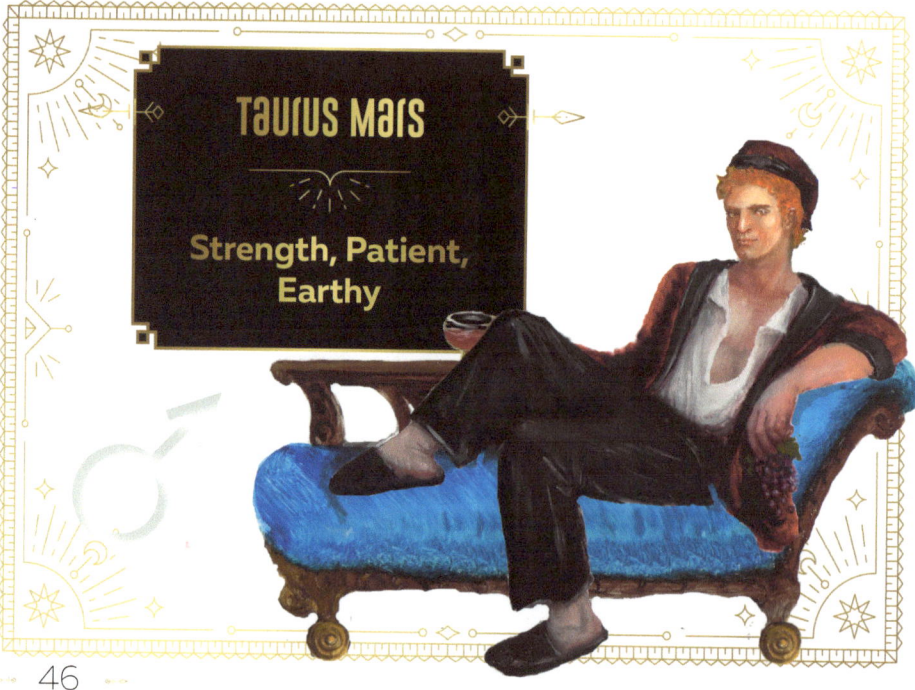

Gemini Mars

Strength, Mobile, Mutable

Cancer Mars

Strength, Nurturing, Emotional

Leo Mars

Strength, Bold, Regal

Virgo Mars

Strength, Careful, Precise

Libra Mars

Strength, Relational, Balancing

Scorpio Mars

Strength, Intense, Private

sagittarius mars

Strength, Expansive, Buoyant

capricorn mars

Strength, Structured, Disciplined

Aquarius Mars

Strength, Tolerant, Progressive

Pisces Mars

Strength, Intuitive, Poetic

Here we see how Jupiter transforms himself through the clothing he wears and the tools he uses in each of the astrological signs. The key word for Jupiter is Fortune.

Aries Jupiter

Fortune, Energetic, Assertive

Taurus Jupiter

Fortune, Patient, Earthy

Gemini Jupiter

Fortune, Mobile, Mutable

Cancer Jupiter

Fortune, Nurturing, Emotional

Leo Jupiter

Fortune, Bold, Regal

Virgo Jupiter

Fortune, Careful, Precise

Libra Jupiter

Fortune, Relational, Balancing

Scorpio Jupiter

Fortune, Intense, Private

sagittarius jupiter

Fortune, Expansive, Buoyant

capricorn jupiter

Fortune, Structured, Disciplined

Aquarius Jupiter

Fortune, Tolerant, Progressive

Pisces Jupiter

Fortune, Intuitive, Poetic

Here we see how Saturn transforms himself through the clothing he wears and the tools he uses in each of the astrological signs. The key word for Saturn is Work.

Aries Saturn

Work, Energetic, Assertive

Taurus Saturn

Work, Patient, Earthy

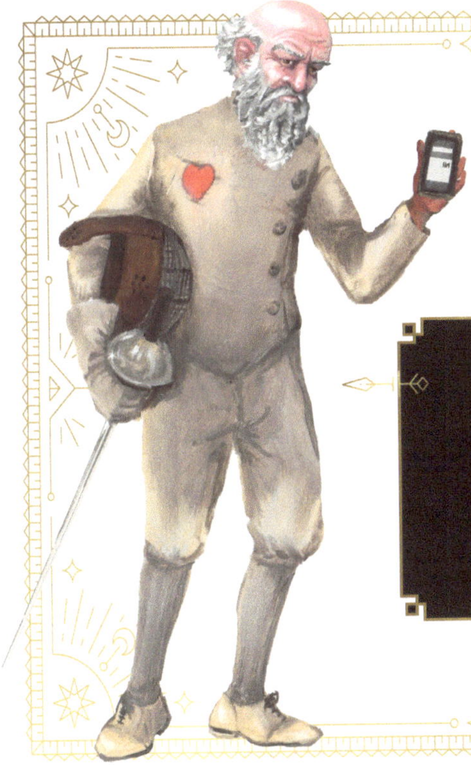

Gemini Saturn

Work, Mobile, Mutable

Cancer Saturn

Work, Nurturing, Emotional

Leo Saturn

Work, Bold, Regal

Virgo Saturn

Work, Careful, Precise

libra saturn

Work, Relational, Balancing

scorpio saturn

Work, Intense, Private

sagittarius saturn

Work, Expansive, Buoyant

capricorn saturn

Work, Structured, Disciplined

aquarius saturn

Work, Tolerant, Progressive

pisces saturn

Work, Intuitive, Poetic

Here we see how Chiron transforms himself through the clothing he wears and the tools he uses in each of the astrological signs. The key word for Chiron is Healing.

Aries Chiron

Healing, Energetic, Assertive

Taurus Chiron

Healing, Patient, Earthy

Gemini Chiron

Healing, Mobile, Mutable

Cancer Chiron

Healing, Nurturing, Emotional

Leo Chiron

Healing, Bold, Regal

Virgo Chiron

Healing, Careful, Precise

libra chiron

Healing, Relational, Balancing

scorpio chiron

Healing, Intense, Private

sagittarius chiron

Healing, Expansive, Buoyant

capricorn chiron

Healing, Structured, Disciplined

aquarius chiron

Healing, Tolerant, Progressive

pisces chiron

Healing, Intuitive, Poetic

Here we see how Uranus transforms itself through the clothing it wears and the tools it uses in each of the astrological signs. The key word for Uranus is Freedom.

Aries Uranus

Freedom, Energetic, Assertive

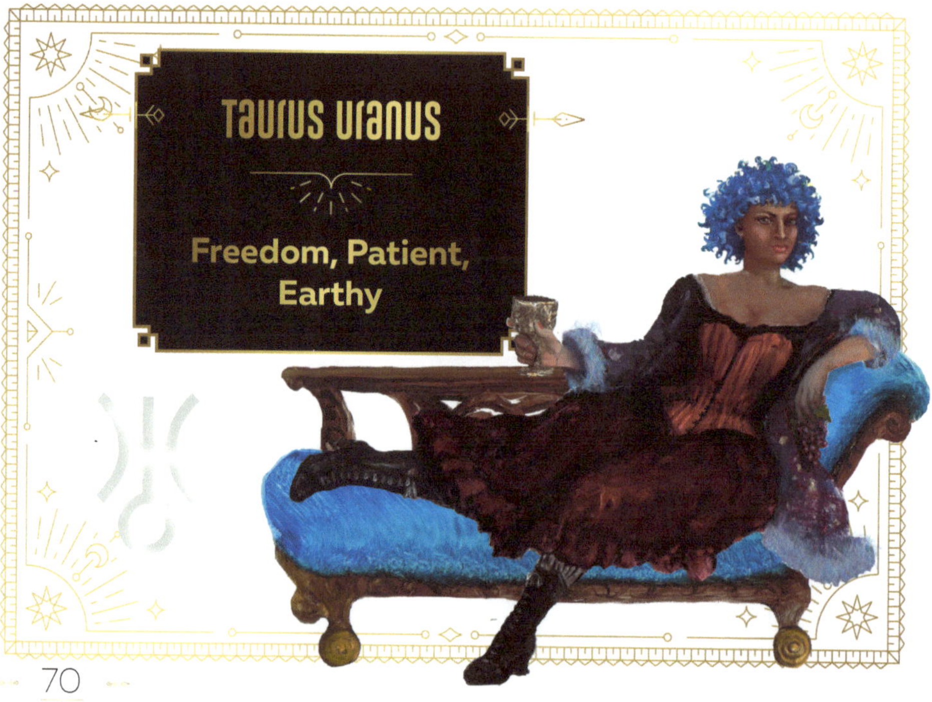

Taurus Uranus

Freedom, Patient, Earthy

Gemini Uranus

Freedom, Mobile, Mutable

Cancer Uranus

Freedom, Nurturing, Emotional

Leo Uranus

Freedom, Bold, Regal

Virgo Uranus

Freedom, Careful, Precise

Libra Uranus

Freedom, Relational, Balancing

Scorpio Uranus

Freedom, Intense, Private

sagittarius uranus

Freedom, Expansive, Buoyant

capricorn uranus

Freedom, Structured, Disciplined

Aquarius Uranus

Freedom, Tolerant, Progressive

Pisces Uranus

Freedom, Intuitive, Poetic

Here we see how Neptune transforms himself through the clothing he wears and the tools he uses in each of the astrological signs. The key word for Neptune is Spirituality.

Aries Neptune

Spirituality, Energetic, Assertive

Taurus Neptune

Spirituality, Patient, Earthy

Gemini Neptune

Spirituality, Mobile, Mutable

Cancer Neptune

Spirituality, Nurturing, Emotional

Leo Neptune

Spirituality, Bold, Regal

Virgo Neptune

Spirituality, Careful, Precise

Libra Neptune

Spirituality,
Relational, Balancing

Scorpio Neptune

Spirituality,
Intense, Private

sagittarius neptune

Spirituality, Expansive, Buoyant

capricorn neptune

Spirituality, Structured, Disciplined

Aquarius Neptune

Spirituality, Tolerant, Progressive

Pisces Neptune

Spirituality, Intuitive, Poetic

Here we see how Pluto transforms himself through the clothing he wears and the tools he uses in each of the astrological signs. The key word for Pluto is Power.

Aries Pluto

Power, Energetic, Assertive

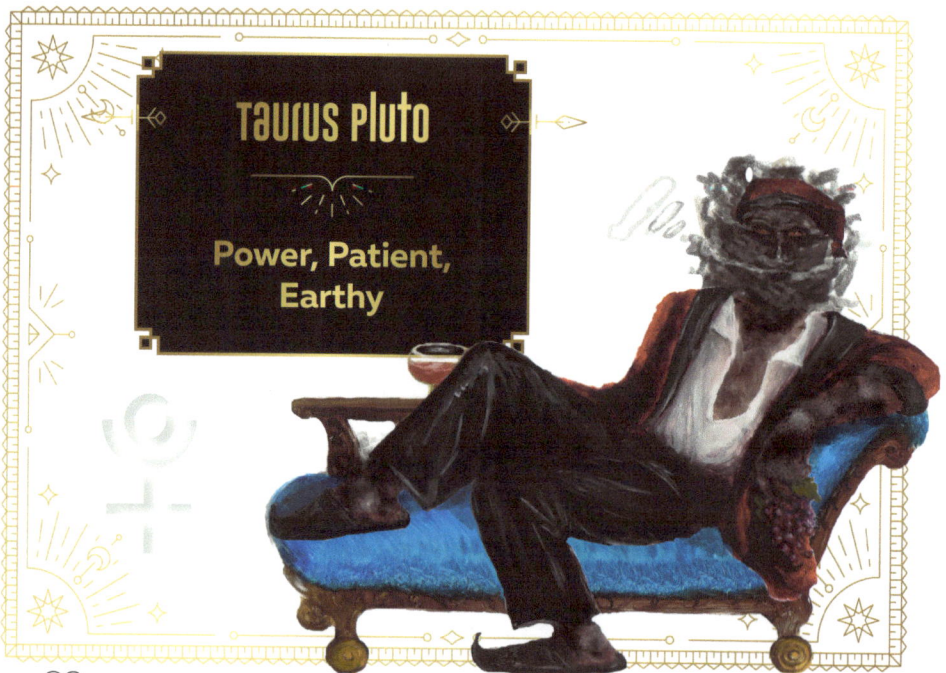

Taurus Pluto

Power, Patient, Earthy

gemini pluto

Power, Mobile, Mutable

cancer pluto

Power, Nurturing, Emotional

Leo Pluto

Power, Bold, Regal

Virgo Pluto

Power, Careful, Precise

Libra Pluto

Power, Relational, Balancing

Scorpio Pluto

Power, Intense, Private

sagittarius pluto

Power, Expansive, Buoyant

capricorn pluto

Power, Structured, Disciplined

aquarius pluto

Power, Tolerant, Progressive

pisces pluto

Power, Intuitive, Poetic

Chapter Three

The Houses or Stages

The Houses represent Stages with two meanings in mind: stages as transition points in our psychological development, and stages as the location where actors perform. Here, we will look at the 12 stages from a developmental perspective, as well as the area in our lives where the action takes place

stage 1

- Developmental Stage:
  Birth

- Areas in Life:
  Birthplace, baby nursery, foyer or dressing room

- Focus:
  Self-image, how the world sees us and how we see the world

- Centering:
  Inner self

stage 2

- Developmental Stage:
  Toddler

- Areas in Life:
  Playroom, vault

- Focus:
  Personal resources, financial, material possessions

- Centering:
  Inner self

stage 3

- Developmental Stage:
  Elementary School

- Areas in Life:
  Neighborhood, siblings

- Focus:
  Communication, activity and the exchange of information and ideas

- Centering:
  Inner self

stage 4

- Developmental Stage:
  Family/Home Life

- Areas in Life:
  Private self behind closed doors, birth family/home

- Focus:
  One's roots, self, ancestry

- Centering:
  Inner other

stage 5

- Developmental Stage:
  Teenager

- Areas in Life:
  Dating/romance, creative spaces

- Focus:
  Self-expression in all its forms: sex, children, art and risk taking

- Centering:
  Inner other

stage 6

- Developmental Stage:
  Adulthood, getting a job

- Areas in Life:
  Work and daily routines

- Focus:
  Service, physical and psychological health, day to day work and duties

- Centering:
  Inner other

stage 7

- Developmental Stage:
  Partnerships

- Areas in Life:
  Relationships

- Focus:
  Significant one to one relationships, partners, enemies

- Centering:
  Outer other

stage 8

- Developmental Stage:
  Commitment/Marriage

- Areas in Life:
  Marriage, death, taxes and inheritance

- Focus:
  Shared resources or resources of others, death and rebirth

- Centering:
  Outer other

stage 9

- Developmental Stage:
  University, higher understanding

- Areas in Life:
  Foreign travel, religion, higher education and philosophy

- Focus:
  Broader viewpoints through travel, religion, philosophy and mental studies

- Centering:
  Outer other

stage 10

- Developmental Stage:
  Career

- Areas in Life:
  Public status

- Focus:
  Public self, position in the world, reputation and vocation

- Centering:
  Self relating to the greater whole

stage 11

- Developmental Stage:
  Old age, retirement

- Areas in Life:
  Associations, groups and allegiances

- Focus:
  Group interactions, friends and associates, social aspirations

- Centering:
  self relating to the greater whole

stage 12

◇│◇ Developmental Stage:
Death, transition beyond the physical

◇│◇ Areas in Life:
One's relationship to God, Goddess or however you define the energy of the All-That-Is.

◇│◇ Focus:
Collective soul, past, that which is hidden, ancestry, devotion to higher ideals and spiritual values, behind the scenes, seclusion

◇│◇ Centering:
Self dissolving into the greater whole

Michael Bartlett focuses on traditional and esoteric astrology while incorporating the depths of the outer planets. His Core Energetic training, highly intuitive nature, three decades of business experience and over two decades of astrological wisdom give him an extensively resourced toolbox he offers to his clients.

Michael is the author of Astrological Mavericks: Do you have what it takes to change the world? A book about individuals with planets on their chart's angles. He offers webinars, workshops, experiential intensives, readings, speaking engagements and co-hosts a weekly YouTube show called Deep Dives with New Perspectives. In addition to being a member of the Board of Trustees, he also offers webinars, workshops and teaches classes for Kepler College. For more information, please visit **coremichael.com**
Facilitating the Change You Seek

www.ingramcontent.com/pod-product-compliance
Lightning Source LLC
Chambersburg PA
CBHW042043290426
44109CB00001B/18